CLAUDIA Schiffer's

Beauty Secrets-From the

Runway to Everyday Life

Linda A. Walker

TABLE OF CONTENTS

INTRODUCTION

Not only a name, Claudia Schiffer is a symbol of classic beauty and refinement. Her transformation into one of the most well-known supermodels in the world from a little German village is evidence of her amazing attraction. Beyond the glitz and glamor of the fashion industry, Claudia has shared her beauty secrets with the globe, encouraging countless people to embrace their charm.

However, Claudia Schiffer represents timeless beauty and grace and is more than just a supermodel. Claudia has discovered the trick to bringing runway glamor into regular life, beyond the cameras and high-fashion catwalks. She's thrilled to share this experience with you since it has given her a profound appreciation of beauty—both within and out.

We encourage you to explore the world of Claudia Schiffer's beauty wisdom in this book, "Claudia Schiffer's Beauty Secrets: From the Runway to Everyday Life." We'll look at how she juggles the responsibilities of everyday life with the glitz and glamor of the runway while still retaining her charm, which is timeless and enthralling.

Embracing the self-assurance, optimism, and well-being that emanates from the inside is at the heart of Claudia's beauty secrets, which go beyond simply having a picture-perfect appearance. Whether it's her morning skincare routine, her simple makeup skills, her commitment to fitness and nutrition, or her dedication to mindfulness and self-care, Claudia's approach to beauty is all-encompassing and doable for anybody looking to improve their natural radiance.

This book explores the essence of beauty as viewed through the eyes of a supermodel who recognizes that true beauty transcends fashion and time and goes beyond cosmetics and skincare. It is not just a manual for these topics. It has been a great journey for Claudia to realize that she feels beauty is a mirror of one's inner self.

We'll delve into Claudia's experiences on the catwalk in the ensuing chapters, revealing the methods and trends in beauty that have influenced the fashion industry. We'll learn about her skincare regimens, cosmetic tricks, and hair care tips that you can apply to your routine. You can follow Claudia's advice whether you're getting ready for a special event or just want to improve your appearance generally.

In contrast to other beauty enthusiasts, Claudia is happy to share her knowledge and insights with you. She does not keep her beauty secrets to herself like priceless artifacts. It's a journey that will, as Claudia Schiffer has done, inspire and empower you to accept your particular beauty.

So, when we start to adhere to standards, it's about recognizing your uniqueness, growing your confidence, and finding the classic elegance that already exists within you. Are you prepared to show off the model-like beauty that's just waiting to shine in your regular life? I'll start now.

CHAPTER 1: WHO IS CLAUDIA SCHIFFER?

The model and actress Claudia Schiffer is from Germany. As one of the most successful models in the world in the 1990s, she soared to popularity and was given the title of supermodel. In addition to Harper's Bazaar, Elle, and Vogue, she has been featured on the covers of over 1,000 magazines. Additionally, she has appeared in advertisements for well-known labels like Chanel, Dior, and Versace.

Schiffer has a background in modeling and has also acted in several films, including Zoolander (2001) and Love Actually (2003). Additionally, she has appeared in Claudia Schiffer: In Her Own Words (2013), a reality television program.

Entrepreneurial and philanthropic success define Schiffer. She founded the Claudia Schiffer Foundation, which supports organizations that benefit children, and she also has her own clothing and accessory business.

Matthew Vaughn, a British film producer, and Schiffer are married; the two of them have three kids. She inspires a lot of people all around the world and is an example for women of all ages.

In addition to her charity efforts, Schiffer is renowned for her classic beauty and sophisticated style. In the fashion world, she is unquestionably an icon.

1.1 Early life and education

On August 25, 1970, Claudia Schiffer, the second youngest of four children, was born in Rheinberg, Germany. She had a lawyer father named Heinz and a housewife mother named Gudrun. Schiffer went to the comprehensive school in his hometown, where he was raised. Despite her average academic performance, she had a lifelong passion for fashion and modeling.

In a Düsseldorf nightclub, a modeling agent spotted Schiffer when she was 17 years old. She immediately became one of the most well-known models in the world and has graced the pages of more than a thousand publications, including Vogue, Elle, and Harper's Bazaar. Additionally, she has appeared in advertisements for well-known labels like Chanel, Dior, and Versace.

Only primary and secondary schools were part of Schiffer's early education. But through her work as a model and businesswoman, she has gained a lot of knowledge. She speaks English, French, and German with ease and is knowledgeable in both business and fashion.

Schiffer's knowledge, beauty, and accomplishments serve as an inspiration to a lot of young girls. In the fashion world, she is unquestionably an icon.

1.2 Claudia's Rise to Supermodel Stardom

Tale of skill, tenacity, and good fortune. Here is a look at how she rose to the top of the fashion industry:

1: Early Life: Claudia Schiffer was born in Rheinberg, Germany, on August 25, 1970. She had an early interest in modeling and had aspirations of being a successful model.

2: Discovery: At the age of 17, Claudia was found at a disco in Düsseldorf, Germany. A modeling agency quickly signed her, which started her professional career.

3: Breakthrough Campaign: Claudia's big break came in 1989 when she was selected as the face of Guess jeans. She became well-known around the world as a result of the seductive black-and-white advertising campaign.

4: Versatile Model: Claudia's versatility as a model allowed her to work with a variety of fashion houses, including Chanel, Versace, Valentino, and Karl

Lagerfeld. She was in high demand because of her versatility in terms of appearance and style.

5: Iconic Vogue Covers: Claudia appeared on the covers of several fashion publications, including Vogue. Her appearances on the Vogue magazine cover cemented her reputation as a supermodel.

6: Cooperation with Karl Lagerfeld: Claudia's career benefited greatly from her close professional association with renowned fashion designer Karl Lagerfeld. She started acting as Lagerfeld's muse and participated in numerous Chanel fashion presentations.

7: Runway Success: Claudia has walked the runway for well-known fashion brands and designers, solidifying her position as one of the top models in the world. She became a runaway favorite due to her tall, statuesque body and dazzling beauty.

8: Global Stardom: By the early 1990s, Claudia Schiffer was well-known all over the world. She was a well-known figure who graced magazine covers and prominent advertising campaigns.

9: Acting Career: Claudia dabbled in acting and made appearances in films including "Love Actually" and "Zoolander." Her venture into acting helped her gain more notoriety.

10: Philanthropic Efforts: In addition to her modeling and acting work, Claudia has supported children's organizations and AIDS research.

11: Legacy: Claudia Schiffer has had a long-lasting influence on both the fashion world and popular culture. She continues to be a legendary figure who has influenced the fashion and cosmetics industries.

Claudia Schiffer's rise from a small German village to one of the most well-known supermodels in the world is a monument to her talent, perseverance, and innate sense of style. Her ascent to supermodel popularity created a lasting impression on the fashion world, and her status as a fashion icon continues to this day.

1:3 The Impact of the Runway on Claudia's Beauty Evolution

For more than three decades, Claudia Schiffer has been regarded as one of the best models in the world. She is renowned for her classic beauty and refined sense of fashion. The runway has had a variety of effects on Schiffer's development as a beauty expert.

First, Schiffer has become familiar with a variety of beauty trends thanks to the runway. She has been able to use this to try out several styles and discover what suits her the best. For instance, Schiffer has experimented with everything from bright lipsticks to natural cosmetics. She has also had a range of hairstyles, from slick bobs to glitzy updos.

Second, the runway has taught Schiffer how to do her hair and cosmetics professionally. She has studied under the world's top hair and makeup specialists. She was able to create her characteristic look with the help of this information.

Third, Schiffer has gained confidence in her looks thanks to the runway. For some of the largest fashion brands in the world, she has walked the runway. She may now show off her beauty to a larger audience thanks to this.

examples of how the runway has influenced Claudia Schiffer's beauty evolution:

1: Early career: The Fresh Face (1980s): Early runway appearances by Claudia in the late 1980s established her as a youthful, fresh-faced model. Her distinctive blonde hair and minimal makeup enhanced her inherent attractiveness.

2: The Supermodel Era (1990s): During the '90s, Claudia, one of the original supermodels, walked the runways of prestigious fashion houses. She embodied the strong, iconic makeup trends of the time, such as matte lips, smokey eyes, and defined brows.

3: Transformative Hairstyles: Claudia frequently underwent risky hairstyle changes while performing on the runway. She effortlessly changed from her traditional long blonde hair to short, stylish bobs and layered cuts, demonstrating her adaptability and versatility as a model.

4: Red Lips and Glamour (2000s): Claudia embraced glamorous looks in the 2000s and emphasized her large lips with red lipstick. Her runway presence continued to develop, fusing traditional beauty with contemporary trends.

5: Timeless Elegance (2010s): Claudia continued to be a fashion star in the 2010s, putting a focus on timeless elegance on the runway. She favored neutral cosmetic colors that emphasized her natural features.

6: Ageless Beautiful (2020): Even when Claudia approached her fifties, her beautiful development inspired many. Her runway appearances demonstrated her timeless beauty and showed that self-assurance and confidence are the real secrets to looking good at any age.

7: Changing Beauty Trends: Throughout her career, Claudia Schiffer has changed the prevailing beauty trends with her runway appearances. Numerous fans and aspiring models copied her distinctive cosmetics and hairdos, which became aspirational.

8: Versatility and Adaptability: Claudia's capacity to acclimatize to a variety of runway styles and beauty looks is a testament to her adaptability as a model. She consistently succeeded in capturing the spirit of the collection, whether the theme was high fashion, boho, or traditional.

9: Confidence and elegance: Claudia's runway beauty progression has been distinguished not just by her physical beauty but also by her intrinsic confidence, elegance, and poise. Her runway outings have constantly highlighted these attributes.

Claudia Schiffer's beauty journey on the runway is a testament to her enduring appeal and her capacity to cross fashion decades. Her transformation from a young model to a timeless beauty legend continues to inspire the fashion and beauty industries, demonstrating the tremendous influence of the runway on her eternal beauty legacy.

CHAPTER 2: THE ART OF CATWALK MAKEUP

A particular kind of makeup, called catwalk makeup, is made to be visible from a distance. It can be used to produce a range of looks, from natural to glamorous, and is frequently bold and dramatic.

Fashionable and attractive makeup looks are a specialty of catwalk makeup artists. They employ a range of methods and materials to produce looks that are both striking and durable.

The base is among the most crucial components of catwalk makeup. Any blemishes or flaws should be hidden, and the skin should be faultless and even. Utilizing a primer, foundation, and concealer will help you achieve this.

The artist will start contouring and highlighting the face once the base has been applied. The features will become more sculpted and defined as a result. To darken the regions where the light would naturally cast shadows on the face, contouring is done with a bronzer or contour powder. To highlight the regions of the face where the sun would normally shine, use a highlighter.

The eyeshadow application is next. Eyeshadow looks that are dramatic and bold are frequently seen on the catwalk. To produce a look that is both trendy and attractive, the artist employs a variety of colors and techniques. The artist might employ a halo eye look, a cat eye look, or a smokey eye look, for instance.

For any catwalk makeup look, eyeliner and mascara are necessary. Eyeliner enhances and defines the eyes, giving them a more dramatic appearance. The eyelashes can be made longer and thicker with mascara.
Applying lipstick is the last step. Lipstick can give the lips a burst of color and finish the catwalk makeup look.

The makeup artist will select a lipstick shade that goes well with the skin tone and eye makeup.

Additional tips for creating a catwalk makeup look:

1: Use high-quality products. This is a further suggestion for developing a catwalk makeup look. It's crucial to use premium products because catwalk makeup is frequently made to endure for hours. This will make it easier to maintain your makeup's best appearance throughout the day or night.

2: Set your cosmetics. Make sure to fix your makeup using a setting powder or spray once you've finished applying it. This will assist in preserving your makeup and prevent it from smudging or fading.

3: Don't be hesitant to try new things. When it comes to makeup for the catwalk, there are no rules. To achieve a look of your love. Don't be afraid to experiment with various colors and styles.

A creative and enjoyable way to express oneself is through catwalk makeup. Consider developing a catwalk makeup look if you want to stand out from the crowd.

2:1 Hairstyles That Define the Fashion Era

Hairstyles have always been a potent representation of cultural, social, and fashion trends. They can serve as a defining characteristic of a particular fashion era. Hairstyles that reflect the social and cultural fads of the moment have come to be recognized as iconic icons of particular historical periods.

Here are a few famous haircuts that are linked to particular fashion eras:

1: The Gibson Girl, from the late 19th through the early 20th century: The Gibson Girl hairstyle, which was distinctive for its voluminous, upswept bun and the use of hairpieces to form an S-shaped curve, represented the fashionable and independent women of the time in the late 19th and early 20th centuries. Charles Dana Gibson's illustrations made this style more well-known.

2: The Bob, from the 1920s: With its angular, straight lines and shorter length, the bob hairstyle came to represent the modern, free-spirited "flapper" women of the Roaring Twenties. It marked a departure from the lengthy, elaborate hairdos of the previous era.

3: Victory Rolls from the 1940s: During the 1940s, particularly during World War II, victory rolls, which are characterized by rolled and curled hair framing the face, were common. The hairdo was named after the Allied triumph, and it captured the nationalistic mood of the day.

4: The Beehive, from the 1960s: The 1960s were known for the beehive, a towering, teased hairstyle. It was renowned for being worn by celebrities like Audrey Hepburn and Dusty Springfield, and it exemplified the spirit of experimentation and defiance of the time.

5: The Afro (the 1970s): Throughout the decade, the black community adopted the Afro hairdo as a symbol of pride and identity. It later became an iconic representation of the time. It was a declaration of cultural empowerment and glorified thick, natural hair.

6: The Punk Mohawk from the 1980s: The punk movement of the 1980s popularized the edgy and rebellious mohawk haircut, which features a strip of upright, frequently vividly colored, and spiked hair down the middle of the head. It was a brazen countercultural declaration.

7: The Rachel from the 1990s: Jennifer Aniston's character Rachel Green on the television show "Friends" made the "The Rachel" haircut, which featured layered, face-framing locks, popular. This hairdo became popular and embodied the '90s style.

8: The Beachy Waves (2000s): The "beachy waves" hairstyle, which is characterized by loose, ruffled waves that give off a relaxed and carefree vibe, became popular in the 2000s. It was related to the era's carefree fashion.

9: The Ombré (2010s): A key hair trend of the 2010s was the ombré, which included a color gradient from dark to light. It represented a blending of creative and natural hair coloring aspects.

10: The Blunt Bob (2020s): The blunt bob, which is characterized by straight, equal-length ends, made a resurgence in the 2020s. It demonstrated a return to simple, streamlined designs.

These haircuts acted as markers of societal and cultural changes in addition to defining their fashion eras. They demonstrate the eternal power of hair as a means of self-expression and a fashion statement by continuing to inspire and have an influence on hairstyling trends today.

2:2 The Influence of Runway Fashion on Beauty Trends

The runway fashion industry has a significant influence on beauty trends. Fashion designers present their most recent collections on the runway, and makeup artists and hairstylists strive to create looks that go well with the clothing. Millions of people throughout the world then witness these styles, and they frequently influence new beauty fads.

The Influence of Fashion Trends from the Runway on Beauty.

1: Creative collaboration: Models, makeup artists, hair stylists, and fashion designers frequently work together on runway presentations. This interplay enables the development of unified looks that stimulate fresh approaches to beauty.

2: Setting the Tone: What we see on the runway affects upcoming seasons. The color schemes, fashion trends, and themes that will rule in terms of beauty and fashion in the upcoming months are hinted at in the collections that are displayed on the catwalk.

3: Bold Statements: Designers use runway presentations to make provocative claims, and hair and makeup are essential components of these claims. Unconventional and avant-garde beauty trends can set off fads that spread into ordinary life.

4: Trendsetting Makeup: On the runway, makeup artists experiment with unusual color schemes, methods, and textures. These experimental cosmetic trends have an impact on the bold eyeshadows and edgy lip colors that are currently in style.

5: Hairstyle Innovation: Runway hairstyles frequently push the envelope and are innovative. Runway hairstyles motivate people to experiment with different hairstyles, whether they are complicated braids, intricate updos, or unusual hair colors.

6. A variety of cultures and historical periods influence fashion designers. Culturally inspired runway beauty looks influence current beauty trends while promoting cultural appreciation.

7: Celebrating Diversity: Models of many ethnicities, body types, and gender identities are now included on the runway, which has become more open. This openness promotes diversity and representation in fashion and beauty.

8: Sustainable Beauty: As environmental responsibility takes center stage in the fashion industry, eco-friendly and sustainable beauty trends develop simultaneously, encouraging pure and ecologically friendly cosmetics.

9: Iconic Moments: Specific runway moments, like the grunge aesthetic of the '90s or Coco Chanel's launch of the little black dress, have had a lasting influence on both fashion and beauty trends.

10: Accessibility: runway looks are now more available than ever thanks to social media and digital fashion shows. Beauty fans may quickly locate tutorials and create at-home versions of looks from the runway.

11: Influential Models: With their iconic looks, models like Kate Moss, Naomi Campbell, and Claudia Schiffer have affected not only beauty ideals and trends but also fashion.

12: Red Carpet Influence: Beauty trends from the runway frequently make an appearance on the red carpet. These trends become even more popular among the general population when celebrities adopt them.

13: Personal Expression: Experimentation and personal expression are encouraged in runway fashion. It encourages creativity by motivating people to see hair and makeup as means of self-expression.

The runway is a dynamic and significant forum for influencing beauty trends. It inspires creativity and innovation in the beauty industry, resulting in wearable designs and avant-garde looks that let people express themselves through hair and makeup in novel and ever-evolving ways.

CHAPTER 3: CLAUDIA'S MORNING ROUTINE FOR RUNWAY - READY SKIN

Claudia Schiffer's flawless skin and ageless attractiveness are examples of her meticulous skincare regimens. Here is a look at Claudia's morning routine for skin that is ready for the runway:

1: Morning Hydration: Claudia hydrates her body from the inside out by having a glass of water first thing in the morning. For good skin, staying hydrated is a crucial first step.

2: mild cleansing: To eliminate any pollutants that might have formed on her skin overnight, she begins her skincare regimen with a mild cleanser. The succeeding phases will have a blank slate thanks to this.

3: Toning: Claudia uses a moisturizing and pH-stabilizing toner after cleansing. Toner can improve the absorption of subsequent products and assist in reestablishing the skin's natural equilibrium.

4: lightweight serum containing antioxidants like vitamin C: She applies this serum. Antioxidants aid in developing a bright complexion by shielding the skin from environmental harm.

5: Eye Cream: To reduce puffiness and dark circles around the eyes, Claudia uses an eye cream. She uses her ring finger to softly tap the product near her eyes.

6: Sunscreen: Claudia's morning regimen is not complete without applying sunscreen. To protect her skin from UV radiation and delay the signs of aging, she chooses a broad-spectrum SPF that has at least an SPF 30 rating.

7: Moisturizer: Claudia finishes with a moisturizing moisturizer to keep her skin soft all day long and lock in moisture. She selects a lightweight product that is appropriate for her skin type.

8: Lip balm: Claudia must take care of her lips. To shield her lips from UV deterioration and maintain their softness, she applies a nutritious lip balm with SPF.

9: Makeup Application: Claudia's makeup application is exact and customized to the day's appearance, whether she's getting ready for the runway or a special function. To have a beautiful, runway-ready image, she collaborates with makeup professionals.

10: A Healthy Diet and Lifestyle: Claudia is aware that skincare goes beyond the use of cosmetics to include a healthy way of life. To promote the general health of her skin, she keeps a balanced diet, exercises frequently, and controls her stress.

11: Self-assurance and mindfulness: Claudia's morning ritual also involves her mind. She embraces a positive outlook and engages in mindfulness practices, which add to her overall glow.

12: Expert Advice: Claudia meets with doctors and skin care specialists to make sure her skincare regimen is adapted to her particular skin's needs and issues,
For her skin to stay youthful and runway-ready.

Claudia Schiffer emphasizes hydration, sun protection, and antioxidant-rich products in her morning routine. Although her skincare regimen is unquestionably efficient, it's crucial to keep in mind that every person has different skin types and demands. You can create a customized program that meets your unique skin objectives by consulting with a skincare expert.

3:1 Evening Skincare For Every day Elegance

Your skincare regimen should feed your skin while you unwind from the day if you want to achieve and retain everyday elegance. Here is a skincare regimen that incorporates rest and efficient skincare techniques for a dash of casual elegance:

1. Start your nightly ritual by delicately taking off your makeup and sunscreen. To make sure all traces of makeup are removed, use gentle micellar water or makeup remover.

2. Double cleansing: Perform a double cleanse after removing your makeup. To remove pollutants, start with an oil-based cleanser, and then use a mild foaming cleanser to completely clean your skin.

3. Exfoliation (1-2 times per week): To remove dead skin cells and encourage skin renewal, exfoliate your skin once or twice per week. To prevent irritation, pick a gentle exfoliator made of natural components.

4. Hydrating Cleansing: Rehydrate your skin by using a hydrating toner or mist as you prepare it for the following procedures.

5. Serums and Treatments: Use serums or treatment products according to the requirements of your skin. These include goods containing active components like retinol, vitamin C, or hyaluronic acid.

6. Eye Cream: To treat issues like puffiness and fine wrinkles, gently pat an eye cream over the sensitive skin around your eyes.

7. Nourishing Moisturizer: Pick a moisturizer that is moisturizing and nourishing for your skin type. For relaxation, gently massage it into your skin in an upward and outward motion.

8. Overnight Mask or Oil (Weekly): For further hydration and renewal, treat your skin to an overnight mask or face oil once per week. These may offer additional moisture and nutrition.

9. Lip Care: Pay attention to how your lips are treated. Before going to bed, moisturize your lips with a lip balm to keep them hydrated and supple.

10. Relaxation Rituals: Spend some time setting up a soothing environment as you go through your skincare routine. To relax, turn on some calming music, light a scented candle, or perform a little mindfulness exercise.

11. Quality Sleep: Give getting a good night's sleep a top priority. A good night's sleep is crucial for skin renewal and regeneration, which benefits your overall skin health.

12. Self-care and confidence: These two qualities are essential to elegance. Knowing that taking care of your

skin is a sign of self-respect, embrace your skincare routine as a kind of self-care.

13. Clean Bedding: To keep your skin clean, change your pillowcases and other bedding frequently because they can collect dirt and oil.

To encourage a sense of casual elegance, this nighttime skincare routine blends efficient skincare treatments with relaxation methods. Keep in mind that the secret to developing and keeping healthy, radiant skin is consistency and using products that are appropriate for your skin type.

3:2 Claudia's Favorite Skincare Products for All Occasions

For more than three decades, Claudia Schiffer has been a supermodel, and she is renowned for her enduring beauty. Her skincare regimen is one of the keys to her skin's radiance. Schiffer uses a variety of Bamford skincare products, but she also has a few go-to items that she keeps on hand for all circumstances.

Here are some of Claudia Schiffer's preferred skincare items for any situation:

1. Bathford Cleansing Balm: This balm cleanses the skin while removing makeup and pollutants in a mild yet effective manner. Shea butter, cocoa butter, and jojoba oil are just a few of the natural oils and butter used to make it.

2. Bamford Refining Exfoliant: This exfoliant gently buffs away dead skin cells from the skin by using bamboo powder. Additionally, chamomile is included to relax and soothe the skin.

3. Hyaluronic acid, which is abundant in the Bamford Face Serum and helps to hydrate and plump the skin, is a key component. Additionally, it contains vitamin C, which improves skin brightness and lessens the visibility of black spots.

4. Bamford Moisturizing Cream: Suitable for all skin types, this cream is creamy and nourishing. Shea butter, cocoa butter, and avocado oil are just a few of the natural oils and butter used to make it.

5. Triple Action Eye Cream: Created to moisturize, brighten, and tighten the delicate skin around the eyes, this eye cream has three main functions. Hyaluronic acid, vitamin C, and peptides are present to help lessen the look of wrinkles and fine lines.

For the healthiest appearance of her skin, Schiffer uses these cosmetics both morning and night. To save her skin from the sun's damaging UV rays, she also uses sunscreen every day.

Schiffer maintains a healthy diet in addition to her skincare regimen to keep her skin glowing. She maintains a healthy diet, consumes lots of water, and exercises frequently. Additionally, she abstains from smoking and consumes too much alcohol.

Claudia Schiffer has been able to keep her ageless beauty for decades by adhering to a constant skincare regimen and leading a healthy lifestyle.

CHAPTER 4: CAPTURING THE RUNWAY LOOK FOR DAILY LIFE

Fashion and makeup trends that are intriguing but not always appropriate for everyday life are frequently shown on the runway. However, you may create more wearable, regular versions of these ensembles by taking inspiration from the runway.

Here's how to translate the runway's spirit into your everyday life:

1: Concentrate on One Bold Element: Runway designs frequently incorporate several striking components, such as eye-catching makeup, dramatic lips, and avant-garde hairstyles. Select one standout piece to emphasize to make the look wearable for daily activities; keep the rest of your makeup and styling understated.

2: Modify Color Intensity: If the runway outfit features bold or unusual hues, think about using softer or more subdued tones for everyday wear. For everyday eyes, choose a more subdued blue or neutral brown if the runway has electric blue eyeshadow, for instance.

3: Simplify Complex Hairstyles: Recreating elaborate runway hairstyles daily can be time-consuming. Simplify them by concentrating on the essential components, like flowing waves or a sophisticated bun, and omitting the minute details.

4: Take Comfort into Account: Runway fashion may include uncomfortably designed or impractical attire. By selecting cozy fabrics, functional footwear, and daily-appropriate styles, you may adapt looks from the runway to your routine.

5: Adapt to Your Environment: Take into account your regular surroundings and activities. For instance, a toned-down version of a runway outfit would be more appropriate than an expensive one if you work in a corporate office.

6: Combine high and low fashion: To achieve the runway vibe, you don't have to dress in expensive gear. To create a look that fits your budget, mix high-fashion goods with reasonably priced and accessible items.

7: Experiment with Accessories: Adding accessories to your outfit is a great way to incorporate trends from the runway. Add bold belts, scarves, or jewelry to your outfit to make it more stylish.

8: Confidence is key. Your best accessory, even while wearing a daring runway style, is confidence.

10: Experiment and Practice: Creating outfits from the runway could take some practice. Try out various makeup applications, haircuts, and clothing combinations until you find a look that suits you.

11: Customize the Look: Add your touches to the runway-inspired ensemble to make it uniquely yours. Whether it's a signature color scheme, a favorite item, or a change in hairdo, inject your personality into the look.

12: Self-Expression: Keep in mind that cosmetics and fashion are both ways of expressing oneself. Feel free to adapt runway components that fit your style and guiding principles.

Finding the right balance between practicality and aesthetic inspiration is key to achieving the runway look in everyday life. While making sure that it fits your lifestyle and comfort, it enables you to add elements of high fashion and originality to your everyday style.

4:1 Claudia's Everyday Magic: Makeup Lips, Cheeks, and Eyes

Claudia Schiffer's classic beauty is frequently described by a sophisticated yet natural makeup style that draws attention to her features without being overdone. Claudia uses the following makeup routine, concentrating on her eyes, lips, and cheeks:

1: Perfect Composition: Claudia begins by moisturizing and cleansing her face. To balance out her skin tone and let her natural beauty show through, she uses a light, dewy foundation or tinted moisturizer.

2: Natural Brows: Claudia has well-groomed, natural-looking eyebrows. She brushes her brows upward for a soft, feathery appearance and lightly fills in any sparse areas with a brow pencil or powder.

3: Subtle Eye Makeup: Claudia chooses earthy and neutral eyeshadow hues that draw attention to her eyes without looking garish. The eyes can be made to appear larger by using a subtle shimmer on the lid and a soft, matte brown or taupe hue in the crease.

4: Defined Lashes: To achieve defined, fluttery lashes, she curls her eyelashes to give them a lift and liberally coats them in mascara. Instead of emphasizing volume, Claudia's everyday style emphasizes length and separation.

5: Simple Eyeliner: Claudia typically wears a thin line of eyeliner along her upper lash line. This draws attention to her eyes without making them appear heavy or smoky.

6: Fresh, Rosy Cheeks: Her cheeks are given a light, rosy blush to give them a healthy flush. The blush is well blended for a youthful glow and a natural appearance.

7: Soft, Natural Lips: Claudia prefers to wear natural lip colors like muted mauves or delicate pinks. For a moisturized appearance, she frequently chooses lipsticks or lip glosses with a satin or glossy finish.

8: Skin-Loving Finishing Touch: Claudia can use a setting spray with a dewy finish to set her makeup and add a hint of radiance. This keeps her makeup in place and preserves her dewy, radiant complexion.

9: Accept Imperfections: Claudia accepts her flaws and stays away from excessive covering. Instead of covering up her innate beauty, her makeup is supposed to highlight it.

10: Timeless Elegance: Claudia's everyday makeup style exemplifies sophistication and timeless elegance. It can be worn in a variety of situations, from more formal events to informal outings.

11: Confidence and self-assurance: Above all, Claudia's confidence and self-assurance fuel her cosmetic magic. Her inner beauty shines through, making her appear effortlessly beautiful in any situation.

Everyday Makeup Magic by Claudia Schiffer emphasizes natural beauty and classic elegance while celebrating simplicity. Her method emphasizes the value of accentuating one's characteristics while embracing uniqueness and confidence, producing a look that is both timeless and alluring.

4.2 Achieving a Signature Look for Any Occasion

Owning a signature look is similar to owning a personal brand that showcases your distinctive sense of fashion and character. Any occasion can benefit from its timeless and adaptable look. The following methods will assist you in developing a signature appearance that is appropriate for every occasion:

1: Identify your style persona: Determine your style persona first. Are you traditional, eclectic, minimalist, or bohemian? The foundation for your unique look will be laid by being aware of your personal style preferences.

2: Clothing necessities: Spend money on classic clothing pieces that go with your sense of style. These may be a sharply fitted blazer, a little black dress, a pair of cozy jeans, or a pair of timeless white shoes.

3: Signature Piece: Take into account an accent or signature piece that characterizes your outfit. It may be a striking piece of jewelry, a hat, or a pair of shoes.

4: Hair and Makeup: Establish a go-to look for your hair and makeup that matches your style. Your beauty regimen should improve your whole appearance, whether it's a classic bun and neutral makeup or beachy waves and bold lips.

5: adaptable outerwear: Select pieces of adaptable outerwear that can be layered over numerous outfits to change the look to suit different weather and events.

6:Confidence is important. You should feel comfortable and confident when wearing your distinctive look. The perfect addition to every look or fashion is confidence.

7: Personal grooming: Take personal grooming seriously. A polished image is enhanced by having well-kept skin, hair, and nails, which adds to your style.

8: Accessorize Carefully: Choose accessories that complement your outfit without being too garish. In terms of accessorizing, less is generally more.

9: Dress for the Occasion: Adapt your characteristic appearance to the particular occasion while keeping it consistent. Add classy accessories to your outfit for formal occasions. Keep it easy and laid back for casual outings.

10: Stay True to Your Style: Even when experimenting with trends, stay true to your sense of style. Instead of adopting styles that feel out of character, incorporate modern features that complement your distinctive style.

11. vary Gradually: Your distinctive appearance can vary, but modifications should be made gradually. This enables you to embrace personal growth and style progression while still maintaining a consistent aesthetic.

12: Confidence and Authenticity: At the end of the day, authenticity and confidence are the keys to a signature appearance. Accept your individuality and let it shine on any given occasion.

Understanding your style, consciously adjusting it, and projecting confidence are the keys to developing a signature appearance that works for any situation. No matter where life takes you, your distinctive style will let people recognize you and appreciate your effortless style.

CHAPTER 5: MAINTAINING HEALTHY AND SHINY HAIR WITH INSPIRATION FROM THE RUNWAY

Long, glossy, and healthy hair can be seen on many runway models. They have a staff of stylists who take good care of their hair and only use high-quality products, which is why With the proper care and practices, you may attain and maintain hair that is healthy, lustrous, and runway-inspired.

This is how:

1. Starting with a proper hair care routine that includes shampooing, conditioning, and occasionally deep conditioning is a good place to start. For your hair's type (dry, oily, curly, or straight) and concerns (dandruff, frizz, or damage), select appropriate items.

2. Minimal Heat Styling: Heat styling products are frequently used for runway looks, but too much heat might harm your hair.

3. Use blow dryers, flat irons, and curling irons sparingly, and always spritz your hair with heat-protectant spray before styling.

4. Cold Water Rinse: Use cold water to rinse your hair after conditioning. This aids in sealing the hair cuticles, giving your hair a glossier appearance, and reducing frizz.

5. Use a Good Hairbrush: Invest in a good hairbrush with natural bristles. It adds shine and keeps hair healthy. Gently brush your hair to distribute natural oils from the scalp to the ends.

6. Shield Your Hair from UV Rays: Shielding your hair from UV rays is just as important as using sunscreen on your skin. When spending time in the sun, put on a hat with a wide brim or use UV-protective hair treatments.

7. Refrain from overwashing your hair because doing so can remove the natural oils from it. Depending on your hair type and degree of exercise, aim to wash your hair every two to three days.

8. Nourishing Hair Masks: To replenish moisture and repair damage, use nourishing hair masks or deep conditioning treatments once per week. Look for products that contain keratin, shea butter, or argan oil.

9. Balanced diet and hydration: Healthy hair is a result of a balanced diet rich in vitamins and minerals. Drink plenty of water and eat things like fruits, vegetables, and proteins that are good for your hair.

10. Avoid Harsh Chemicals: Use sulfate- and paraben-free, mild hair products as little as possible. Choose sulfate-free shampoos and conditioners to avoid removing the natural oils from your hair.

11. Regular haircuts: To keep your hair healthy and in good shape while removing split ends, get regular haircuts every 6 to 8 weeks.

12. Silk Pillowcase: Using a silk pillowcase while you sleep will lessen friction and hair damage. Additionally, it keeps your hair looking smoother and aids in maintaining your hairstyle.

13. Stress management: Excessive stress might harm your hair's health. Use stress-reduction methods like yoga or meditation to enhance overall wellness, which will show in the shine of your hair.

14. Steer clear of tight hairstyles. Tight hairstyles like braids or ponytails might damage your hair. Use hair-friendly accessories and looser hairstyles.

15. Consistency is key. It takes time and consistency to achieve and maintain healthy, lustrous hair. You'll gradually see benefits if you follow a hair care regimen that works for you.

With the proper care and attention, it is possible to get runway-inspired, healthy, and shiny hair. You may have hair that glows with health and vitality, just like the models on the runway, by incorporating these methods into your daily hair care routine.

5:1 Iconic Hairstyles That Transition from Runway to Reality

Although the hairstyles on the runway are frequently artistic and avant-garde, they can serve as an inspiration for simple, everyday appearances that are fashionable and useful. Here are some well-known catwalk-inspired hairstyles that work just as well in everyday life:

1: Beachy Waves: The traditional beachy wave hairdo is always stylish and appropriate for any situation. Use a curling wand to make loose, unforced waves to replicate the style. It's a look that works well for both more laid-back outings and formal occasions.

2: Sleek Low Ponytail: This style of ponytail radiates elegance and simplicity. This classic hairstyle is adaptable for any situation because it can be dressed up or down. To obtain a smooth finish, use a hair gel or serum.

3. Messy Bun: A favorite of the runway, the messy bun is ideal for hurried mornings or informal days. It keeps your hair out of your face and gives your appearance a hint of effortlessness.

4: Half-Up, Half-Down: This hairstyle combines the best features of both worlds. It is useful for keeping hair out of your face and displays lovely flowing strands. For a fashionable twist, add a few twists or braids.

5: Blunt Bob: The blunt bob is a stylish, current haircut that is incredibly functional for daily life. It can be tailored to your favorite length and style and requires little care.

6: Fishtail Braid: This runway staple may be dressed up or down, depending on the situation. They enhance your appearance with a touch of elegance and look fantastic on both long and medium-length hair.

7: Classic Updo: For weddings, galas, and other special occasions, a classic updo, such as a French twist or chignon, is a timelessly elegant option. It is elegant, refined, and high-fashion-inspired.

8: High Ponytail: A high ponytail gives you a polished, put-together look. When dressed elegantly and voluminously, it's perfect for a night out, a business meeting, or even a workout.

9: Curtain Bangs: Curtain bangs give your face tenderness by offering versatility and flattery. They nicely frame your features and can be fashioned in a variety of ways to fit various situations.

10: The pixie cut is daring, stylish, and remarkably low-maintenance. It's a runway-inspired look that you can wear every day to stand out.

11: Classic Curls: Whether tight or loose, classic curls are a classic option for a clean and classy appearance. To obtain this sophisticated look, use a curling iron or hot rollers.

12: Effortless Side Part: A side part can instantly update your appearance and lend it a more sophisticated feel. This look is simple to accomplish and suitable for a variety of events, regardless of whether you have long or short hair.

These recognizable runway-inspired hairstyles are adaptable to your lifestyle and preferences, making them practical choices for daily living. There is a hairstyle on the runway that is ideal for you, regardless of whether you favor the effortless and casual look or the polished and sophisticated look.

CHAPTER 6: CLAUDIA'S APPROACH TO EVERYDAY FITNESS

Because she has always led a fit and healthy lifestyle, Claudia Schiffer possesses timeless beauty and a general sense of well-being.

Here are some of her exercise routine

1: Regular Exercise: Claudia works exercise into her daily schedule. This consists of a combination of aerobic, weightlifting, and flexibility exercises.

2: Diverse activities: To keep things new and test various muscle groups, she participates in a range of activities. Yoga, Pilates, swimming, and even outdoor pursuits like cycling and hiking are included in this.

3: Balanced Diet: Claudia consumes a healthy, balanced diet. She probably makes sure her meals contain a range of fruits, vegetables, lean meats, whole grains, and healthy fats. Additionally, it is crucial to remain hydrated.

4: Portion Control: Keeping your portions in check is essential for controlling your caloric intake. Claudia emphasizes eating thoughtfully and in moderation.

5: Getting Enough Sleep: Sleep and recovery are essential for physical health and overall well-being. Getting enough sleep and giving her body time to recover from workouts are priorities for Claudia.

6: Keeping Active Every Day: Claudia makes physical activity a part of her everyday routine. This involves moving around while participating in hobbies, walking instead of using the elevator, and going for walks.

7: Mind-Body Connection: Claudia places a high value on mindfulness and mental health. Exercises in deep breathing or meditation can enhance physical fitness.

8: Expert Advice: Claudia, like many people who are committed to exercise, seeks advice from fitness experts, personal trainers, or nutritionists to make sure her program is in line with her goals and upholds her general health.

9: Setting Achievable and Sustainable Goals Claudia sets attainable and sustainable long-term fitness goals. This keeps her focused and motivated.

10: Staying Active with Family: Claudia makes staying active with her family an enjoyable experience. Sports and family outings may help everyone live a healthy lifestyle.

11: Flexibility and Adaptability: Claudia has a flexible workout regimen that can adjust to her schedule and take into account unforeseen changes because she is aware that life can be busy.

12:Embracing enjoyable things: When you participate in things you enjoy, staying healthy may be fun. Claudia makes fitness a lasting part of her lifestyle by selecting exercises and physical pursuits that she enjoys.

While Claudia Schiffer's approach to exercise might serve as an example, it's important to keep in mind that every person's fitness program is unique. Finding a fitness regimen that your objectives, interests, and lifestyle while taking into account your particular requirements and preferences is essential because what works for one person may not work for another.

6:1 Nutrition Tips for Daily Radiance

Your diet has a vital role in generating everyday radiance, which is essential for maintaining a healthy and glowing appearance from the inside out. To help you nourish your body and skin for a radiant complexion, here is some nutrition advice.

1: Drink Enough Water: To properly hydrate, start each day with a glass of water. Drinking plenty of water keeps your skin looking moisturized and keeps toxins out of your system.

2: Consume a Rainbow of Fruits and Vegetables: Make an effort to include a range of fruit and vegetable dishes that are vibrant in color each day. Antioxidants, vitamins, and minerals found in abundance in these foods support healthy skin and fight free radicals.

3: Omega-3 Fatty Acids: Include foods high in omega-3 fatty acids in your diet, such as flaxseeds, walnuts, and fatty fish (such as salmon and mackerel). Omega-3 fatty acids support the moisture and suppleness of the skin.

4: Lean Proteins: Include lean protein-rich foods in your diet, such as poultry, fish, tofu, and lentils. Protein promotes the synthesis of collagen, which is necessary for skin suppleness.

5: Consume sources of healthy fats, such as nuts, avocados, and extra virgin olive oil. Your skin benefits from these lipids, which also aid in preserving its natural hydration.

6: foods High in Antioxidants: Berries, green tea, dark chocolate, and almonds are full of antioxidants that shield your skin from free radical damage and support a clear complexion.

7: Whole Grains: Opt for whole grains instead of refined grains, such as oats, quinoa, and brown rice. Your skin can benefit from whole grains because they help balance blood sugar levels and supply critical nutrients.

8: Foods that Boost Collagen: Foods high in vitamin C, such as citrus fruits, strawberries, and bell peppers, aid in the body's production of collagen, a protein that is essential for the health of your skin.

9: Reduce Your Consumption of Processed Foods: Cut back on your intake of processed foods, sugary snacks, and sugary beverages. These can cause accelerated aging and skin problems, including acne.

11: Green, leafy vegetables: Include leafy greens in your diet, such as spinach and kale. They are abundant in vitamins A and C, which support healthy skin and offer sun protection.

12: Sufficient Fiber: A diet rich in fiber supports gut health, which is related to skin health. Whole grains, legumes, fruits, and vegetables are examples of foods high in fiber.

13: Steer clear of excessive salt intake, which can cause puffiness and water retention. Reduce your salt intake and season your food with herbs and spices instead.

14: Foods High in Probiotics: Probiotics help maintain a healthy gut microbiome, which can help with acne and eczema. They are present in yogurt, kefir, sauerkraut, and kimchi.

15: Balanced Meals: fats, complex carbohydrates, and lots of veggies. Your skin can get a variety of nutrients from balanced meals.

16: Portion Control: Watch your intake to maintain a healthy weight because a rapid weight increase might harm your skin.

It's important to keep in mind that the secret to daily radiance lies not only in what you eat but also in how frequently you provide your body with a range of healthy foods. You may acquire and keep up a beautiful complexion by using the right skincare products, healthy eating habits, and frequent exercise.

CHAPTER 7: MINDFULNESS AND INNER PEACE FOR EVERYDAY LIVING

mindfulness is a technique for being conscious of your ideas, feelings, and physical sensations while avoiding becoming sucked into them. An internalized feeling of serenity and tranquility is known as inner peace. It is a sensation of harmony with oneself and the environment.

Meditation, yoga, and tai chi are just a few examples of the disciplines that can help you develop mindfulness and inner calm. Even if you don't have much time, you can still put them into practice in your daily life. Here are some pointers:

1: Morning mindfulness routine: Spend some time in the present moment before you begin your day. You can meditate, practice deep breathing, or just sit quietly and consider your goals for the day.

2: Mindful Breathing: Take breaks to practice mindful breathing throughout the day. As you slowly and thoroughly breathe in and out, pay attention to your breath. This assists in stress reduction and mental calmness.

3: Mindful Eating: Give your meals your undivided attention. Consider the flavors, textures, and fragrances in each bite. While eating, stay away from distractions like phones and TV.

4: Grounding Techniques: Use these when you're feeling stressed or overwhelmed. To ground yourself in the present, feel your feet on the ground, touch something, or take a moment to look at yourself.

5: thoughtful walking: Even if it's simply around your house or place of employment, go for brief, thoughtful walks. Pay attention to your surroundings, your surroundings' sounds and sights, and your every step.

6: Practice gratitude by listing your blessings daily. This routine helps promote inner tranquility by changing your emphasis to the positive.

7: Mindful Listening: Engage in active listening throughout conversations. Truly listen to what others are saying without passing judgment or pre-planning responses.

8: Acceptance and non-judgment are important concepts to include in your daily life. Give up the impulse to continually assess or judge others and yourself.

9: Mindful Work: Take a mindful approach to your work. Avoid multitasking because it can cause tension and distraction. Instead, concentrate on one task at a time and give it your complete attention.

10: Evening Reflection: Think back on your day before you go to sleep. Think about the positive aspects, the lessons you learned, and any happy or peaceful times. As you get ready for sleep, let go of any anxieties or worries.

11:Technology Use with Mindfulness: Use technology with awareness. Establish specific hours for monitoring social media and email, and restrict screen time before bed.

12: Nature Connection: Whenever you can, spend time in nature. You can have a deep sense of tranquility in nature, which can also make you feel rooted and connected.

13: Mindful Relationships: Be mindful when interacting with family and friends.
Communicate with awareness, empathy, and compassion.

14: Self-Compassion: Work on your compassion. being kind and sympathetic towards others when they struggle, falter, or feel inadequate.

15: Consider incorporating guided meditation into your daily routine. Numerous online tools and apps provide guided sessions.

Every area of your daily life can incorporate the practice of mindfulness. It's about developing a keener awareness of the present moment and experiencing each moment with openness and interest. It doesn't require a unique environment or extended periods. With practice, mindfulness can help you experience greater inner calm, resiliency, and contentment in your daily life.

7:1 Claudia's Wellness Rituals for Everyday Balance.

Supermodel, actress, and businesswoman Claudia Schiffer is renowned for her classic beauty and active lifestyle. She attributes achieving and maintaining her general well-being to her wellness practices.

Here are a few of Claudia Schiffer's daily wellness practices for harmony:

1: Morning Meditation: A little meditation session might help you get a good start on the day. To center her thoughts and intentions, Claudia practices mindfulness or guided meditation.

2: A Filling Breakfast: A filling breakfast is crucial. For a balanced supper that would provide her with the energy she needed for the day, Claudia chose foods like whole grains, proteins, and healthy fats.

3: Exercise and movement: Regular exercise is essential to good health. Whether it's a morning yoga class, a gym workout, or a nature stroll, Claudia works out every day.

4: Mindful Eating: Claudia practices mindful eating by taking her time with each bite and focusing on her body's signals of hunger and fullness.

5: Hydration: hydration is important for good health. She has a glass of water when she gets up and keeps drinking all day.

6: Skincare and self-care: Having a skincare routine can be a way to take care of yourself. In Claudia's skincare routine, cleansing, moisturizing, and sun protection are all included.

7: The Nature Connection: Being in nature rejuvenates you. Whether it's a walk around the garden or a hike across the countryside, Claudia takes breaks to enjoy the outdoors.

8: Gratitude Journaling: Claudia keeps a gratitude diary and uses it to reflect on her daily blessings and foster thankfulness.

9: Creating time between work and personal life is essential. She establishes limits to make sure she has time for her loved ones, friends, and leisure.

10 : Creative outlets: Engaging in artistic, musical, or literary endeavors can help people feel better emotionally. Claudia uses her creative talents as a way to express herself.

11: Quality Family Time: Making time for your family is important. She plans times for them to connect and bond.

12: Mindful Breathing Breaks: To keep calm and reduce stress, Claudia takes mindful breathing breaks throughout the day.

13: Evening Wind-Down: Before going to bed, you should unwind. She reads, listens to peaceful music, or practices relaxation techniques as calming activities. Claudia has appropriate sleep hygiene, which makes for a peaceful night's sleep.

14: Constant Learning: Continuous learning and personal development can enhance happiness. She engages in reading, workshops, or the pursuit of novel hobbies.

Wellness rituals are highly individualized and might differ from person to person; it's vital to remember that. Finding practices that speak to you and encourage balance and well-being in your own life is crucial. Like Claudia Schiffer and other wellness-conscious people, you may develop a daily routine that promotes your physical and mental health by giving self-care a high priority, practicing mindfulness, and fostering diverse elements of well-being.

7:2 Embracing Well-Being in the Daily Routine

It can be difficult to achieve a sense of well-being while juggling the responsibilities of daily living, but it's necessary for a happy and healthy existence. Here are some tips to assist you in striking a balance between your everyday obligations and your well-being:

1: Make self-care a priority. Make taking care of yourself a priority in your daily routine. Set aside time to engage in rejuvenating pursuits, such as reading, meditation, bathing, or simply relaxing with a cup of tea.

2: Create healthy limits: Define limits between your personal life, your career, and your downtime. To prevent burnout, don't overcommit and develop the ability to say no when it's necessary.

3: Practice Mindfulness: Develop mindfulness by being observant of the current moment. You may improve your general well-being and manage stress by using mindfulness practices like deep breathing and meditation.

4: Maintain a balanced meal: Consume a nutritious, well-balanced meal that gives your body the critical nutrients it needs. A body that is properly fed can handle stress and other obstacles better.

5: Regular Exercise: regular exercise in your daily routine includes. Endorphins are released during exercise, which lowers tension and improves mood.

6: Get Enough Sleep: Make sleep a top priority by striving for 7-9 hours of restful sleep each night.

7: Time Management: Effective time management will help you complete duties more quickly while freeing up time for leisure and other activities.

8: Assign tasks and request assistance. Don't be afraid to assign tasks or request assistance when necessary.

Embrace a network of people who can help you manage your duties.

9: Pursue Interests and Hobbies: Take part in pursuits that make you happy and complete you. These activities allow for emotional release and help lessen stress.

10: Stay Connected: Continue to stay in touch with family and friends. Social support is essential for maintaining emotional health.

11: Learn to Let Go: Let go of the urge for control and excellence. Realizing that some things are out of your control and learning to let go might help you feel less stressed and anxious.

12: Schedule Regular Breaks: Plan brief rest periods throughout the day. Stretching or deep breathing for even a short while can help.

13: Embrace flexibility. Things can change in life. Be adaptable and flexible in your expectations and plans.

14: Seek Professional Help: Don't be afraid to contact a therapist or counselor for help if you're feeling overburdened or experiencing mental health problems.

15: thankfulness Practice: Develop a practice of thankfulness by considering the good things in your life. This may cause you to reorient your attention to happiness and well-being.

To successfully balance daily life and well-being, one must be self-aware and persistent in their efforts. Keep in mind that your health comes first, and you may give yourself a healthier and more balanced existence by using these techniques.

CHAPTER 8: INCORPORATING RUNWAY STYLES INTO EVERYDAY FASHION

Although runway fashion frequently has an ostentatious and avant-garde appearance, you may easily incorporate aspects of the runway into your regular wardrobe. Here's how to incorporate runway trends into your regular wardrobe:

1: Statement Accessories: Add flair to your casual attire with statement accessories like spectacular belts, jewelry, or big sunglasses. These striking accents can completely change a plain outfit.

2: Combine High and Low: Combine expensive designer products with more reasonably priced items. This fusion of high design and affordable clothing results in a fashionable and distinctive look.

3: Have fun with color. Try out bold and unusual color combinations. Don't be afraid to mix and match hues to create eye-catching outfits because runway design frequently favors bright hues.

4: Bold Prints and Patterns: Adopt striking prints and patterns, including florals, animal prints, and geometric shapes. For a dash of runway flair, incorporate them into your attire, shoes, or accessories.

5: Tailored Pieces: Invest in jackets, pants, and blouses that are well-tailored basics. These classic items may be dressed in a variety of ways and lend a touch of sophistication to any outfit.

6: Monochromatic Looks: Use several tones of a single color to create monochromatic ensembles. This style statement can be strong with this modest approach.

7: Layering: Try out different combinations of textures and materials to layer. Layering your clothing can give it depth and appeal.

8: Exaggerated and Playful Silhouettes: Try dressing in exaggerated and playful silhouettes like oversized sweaters, wide-leg jeans, or billowy sleeves. These can give your outfit drama and a modern touch.

9: Trends Inspired by the Runway: Keep up with the latest trends in fashion and adopt runway-inspired looks that suit your taste. Adding these components to your collection, whether they be capes, metallic fabrics, or fringed embellishments, can maintain your appearance.

10: Strategically accessorize: Pick items that go with the runway mood you're going for. A chic handbag, a current belt bag, or a bold pair of boots will quickly improve your ensemble.

11: Use Special Materials: Include distinctive fabrics in your clothing, such as leather, velvet, or metallics. These materials can add an opulent touch to your clothing.

12: Mix casual and fancy: To achieve a balanced style, mix clothes that are both casual and fancy. For a sleek contrast, wear sneakers with a fitted blazer or a denim jacket with a chic skirt.

13: Confidence Is Important: Possessing confidence is essential for pulling off runway-inspired looks. You'll naturally exude style if you dress in whatever makes you feel confident and at ease.

14: Create Your Look: Tailor looks from the runway to suit your taste. Make them appear like you by personalizing them according to your tastes.

15: Take fashion chances: Don't be scared to venture outside of your comfort zone and take fashion chances. Fashion is about expressing oneself, so embrace innovation and originality.

Finding inspiration and modifying it to fit your lifestyle and personality are the keys to incorporating runway trends into your everyday wardrobe. You may create distinctive and fashionable ensembles that represent your sense of style and stand out in any environment by incorporating runway fashion components into your everyday wardrobe.

8:1 Wardrobe Essentials for Everyday Glamour

It is not necessary to have an abundance of expensive clothing to achieve everyday glamor. Instead, it's about having a variety of adaptable wardrobe staples that enable you to effortlessly appear and feel great.

Here are some examples to think about:

1: Little Black Dress (LBD): A timeless option for every event, a black dress is always in style. Choose a style that can be dressed up or down with accessories and flatters your body type.

2: Tailored Blazer: A blazer that fits you perfectly instantly makes you look better. For versatility, go for a neutral hue like gray, black, or navy.

3: Crisp White Button-Up Shirt: A crisp white shirt is a stylish and elegant option. It can be worn with jeans for a more laid-back appearance or with a skirt or pants for a dressier effect.

4: Well-fitted Jeans: Spend money on a pair of upscale, properly fitted jeans. Dark wash jeans may be dressed up with heels or down with shoes, thanks to their adaptability.

5: Pencil Skirt: A pencil skirt is a chic and flattering garment that can be dressed up or down, depending on the situation.

6: Statement Heels: A pair of statement heels, like strappy sandals or classic pumps, will instantly glam up any ensemble.

7: Little Red Dress: Just as necessary as the LBD, a little red dress gives your outfit a splash of color and a boost of self-assurance.

8: Trench Coat: A timeless trench coat is both fashionable and practical. It's ideal for spiffing up your outerwear.

9: Tailored Trousers: Spend money on a pair of stylish, neutral-colored trousers. They can be worn with blazers or blouses for a refined appearance.

10: Silk Blouse: A silk blouse gives your clothing a touch of luxury. It looks great when worn with skirts, pants, or jeans.

11: Statement Jewelry: Bold necklaces and exquisite earrings are two examples of statement jewelry that can instantly upgrade your appearance.

12: Classic Handbag: Invest in a premium, timeless handbag in a basic shade. It ought to be adaptable enough to go with a variety of clothes.

13: Wrap Dress: A wrap dress may be dressed up with accessories or worn simply, and it is universally flattering.

14:Timeless Outerwear: For extra glitz and warmth, think about a cashmere coat or a leather jacket as timeless outerwear options.

15: High-Quality Basics: Spend money on high-quality essentials like cozy t-shirts, a camisole that fits well, and seamless

16: underwear. These provide a sturdy base for your ensembles.

17: Confidence: The key component of casual elegance is confidence. You'll exude glamor from the inside out if you wear your clothes with pride.

The key to everyday glamor is to look and feel your best. These wardrobe necessities give you a strong basis for putting together dazzling ensembles that fit your lifestyle and give you a sense of beauty and confidence in any setting.

8:2 Dressing with Confidence Every Day

Choosing clothes that make you feel good about yourself is essential to dressing confidently every day. It's also important to know how to dress in a way that complements your personality and body type.
The secret to always feeling and looking your best is confidence. Here are some pointers to help you look confident when you dress:

1: Know Your Style: Recognize your style and what makes you feel most confident and at ease. Accept it, whether it's traditional, bohemian, edgy, or eclectic.

2: Dress well-fitted: Wearing clothing that is well-fitted and flatters your body form can give you more confidence. Think about having clothing customized for the best fit.

3. Create a Versatile Wardrobe: Fill your wardrobe with adaptable items that you can mix and match with ease. This makes it simple for you to put together fashionable outfits.

4: Dress Appropriately: Make sure your attire is acceptable for the event. You'll feel more at ease and confident if you dress according to the occasion or environment.

5: Embrace Color: Have fun with color, and don't be scared to try new things. Select hues that are vivid for you and go well with your skin tone.

6: Highlight Your Best Features: Draw attention to your best qualities. Choose skirts or dresses if you enjoy showing off your legs. Off-the-shoulder tops are a great option if you love your shoulders.

7: Quality over quantity: Spend your money on high-quality apparel rather than a lot of cheap clothing. Many times, high-quality items fit better and last longer.

8: Wear layers: Layering gives your clothing depth and interest. You can blend patterns, colors, and textures, which can give you more confidence.

9: Accessorize Carefully: Pick up items that complement your appearance and attitude. They may serve as conversation openers and self-esteem builders.

10: Put Comfort First: Wear comfortable clothing made of materials that feel nice against your skin. Being physically at ease makes it simpler to project confidence.

11: Prepare: Choose your clothes the night before. By doing this, you can avoid the morning rush and make sure you dress flatteringly.

12: Self-Care Matters: Give self-care, such as skincare, haircare, and grooming, a high priority. Feeling presentable improves your level of confidence in general.

13: Mindset matters. Develop an optimistic outlook. Instead of obsessing over your apparent shortcomings, concentrate on your accomplishments and qualities.

14: Stand tall: Your posture has a big impact on how confident you come across. Make eye contact, walk purposefully, and stand tall.

15: Practice makes perfect. You'll become more confident in your fashion selections the more you experiment with various looks and styles.

16: Trust your instincts. Wear what makes you feel good. Trust your fashion instincts. Speaking your truth helps you gain confidence.

17: Take Advice from Others: Look to style icons or other people you respect for inspiration. Include components that speak to you.

It takes work to dress with confidence, and it starts with feeling comfortable with yourself. Your clothes should convey your personality and give you confidence. Dressing with confidence makes you look amazing and exudes a pleasant vibe that can uplift others and make your day.

CHAPTER 9: TIME - EFFICIENT BEAUTY TIPS FOR BUSY LIVES

It is not necessary to spend a lot of time on your beauty routine. Here are some quick beauty tips for those with busy lives:

1: Multipurpose Skincare: Choose skincare items with various uses, like a moisturizer with SPF. This streamlines your process and saves time.

2: Invest in a Good Concealer: You can avoid applying foundation to your entire face by using a quality concealer to swiftly hide blemishes, dark circles, and other flaws.

3: Dry Shampoo: Dry shampoo can add volume and rejuvenate your hair in only a few minutes, allowing you to go longer between thorough washes.

4: Simplify Your Makeup Routine: For everyday wear, stick to a straightforward makeup routine. To seem put-together and fresh, pay attention to necessities like lip balm, mascara, and a hint of blush.

5: Create a tiny makeup bag with your daily necessities so you can put on makeup on the fly if necessary.

6: Learn a few quick hairstyles that you can put together in a matter of minutes, such as a messy bun, a ponytail, or some quick braids.

7: Use tinted lip balms instead of lipstick and lip balm individually by adding color and hydration to your lips in one easy step.

8: Keep makeup remover wipes close at hand because they make it easy to rapidly wash your face after a long day.

9: Weekly Beauty Routine: Set aside a certain time each week for longer beauty regimens, such as deep conditioning your hair, exfoliating, or using a face mask.

10: Make skincare a priority. Pay special attention to keeping your complexion bright so that you won't need to wear as much makeup.

11. Select Low-Maintenance Hairstyles: Take into account low-maintenance cuts and styles that demand little styling and care.

12: Streamline Your Closet: Having a well-organized closet with pieces that can be worn in a variety of ways makes it simpler to swiftly put together fashionable ensembles.

13: Make a plan. To save time in the morning, lay out your clothes and accessories the night before.

14: Regular Maintenance: To preserve a well-groomed appearance without spending too much time at the salon, regularly cut your hair and nails.

15: Accept Imperfections: Accept flaws and embrace your inherent beauty. By adopting this attitude, you can save time and gain confidence.

16: Drink Plenty of Water and Sleep Enough: Proper hydration and enough sleep promote a healthy complexion, which lessens the need for heavy makeup.

17: Delegate When Possible: To save time, think about outsourcing some beauty procedures, such as obtaining a professional haircut or scheduling a spa day.

Being confident and at ease in your skin is what beauty is all about. Even on the busiest days, you may look and feel your best without spending a lot of your important time if you follow these time-saving beauty suggestions.

9:1 Quick Beauty Fixes for Everyday Occasions

These simple cosmetic treatments can save the day when you're short on time but still want to look your best for casual occasions:

1: Use a moisturizing facial spray to refresh your skin. This will give you a healthy glow and instantly rejuvenate your dull skin. Keep a small bottle of perfume in your bag for short spritzes all day.

2: Concealer for Instant Brightening: Apply concealer to blemishes and under-eye circles to instantly cover imperfections and look more awake.

3: Lip Balm with a Tint: A tinted lip balm gives your lips moisture and a hint of color, instantly boosting your appearance.

4: Dry Shampoo for Hair Volume: When you don't have time for a full wash, spray some dry shampoo at the roots of your hair to absorb extra oil and add volume.

5: Mascara for Eye Definition: Applying mascara quickly can open up your eyes and give you a more awake, polished appearance.

6: Apply a clear or colored brow gel to your brows to tame unruly brows and give them a finished appearance.

7: Blush for a Healthy Flush: Use a blush that looks natural to instantly give your cheeks a healthy flush of color.

8: Quick Hair Accessory: You may put up a stunning appearance with little effort by using hair accessories like clips, headbands, or scrunchies.

9: Roll-On Perfume: Roll-on perfumes are practical for an instant aroma upgrade. For a delicate aroma, apply it to your pulse points.

10: Face Wipes for a Clean Slate: Keep facial cleansing wipes on hand as a quick method to take off makeup and revitalize your face.

11: Use Eye Drops to Brighten Your Eyes: If you have weary or red eyes, use eye drops to rapidly brighten and calm them.

12: Quick Nail Touch-Up: To renew your manicure and add gloss, paint your nails with a clear top coat.

13: Carry a stain-removing pen or some wipes with you to deal with spills or stains on your outfit right away.

14: Portable Hairbrush/Comb: On the go, you may tame unruly hair with the aid of a small, foldable hairbrush or comb.

15: Instant Teeth Whitening: For an immediate refreshing and brightening effect, chew sugar-free gum or use teeth-whitening strips.

16: Cooling eye masks: Use cooling eye masks to relieve puffiness and revive weary eyes if you have a minute.

17: Emergency Kit: Create a compact beauty emergency kit with necessary items like hair ties, transparent nail paint, safety pins, and a small sewing kit for unforeseen circumstances.

Even when you're short on time, these quick beauty treatments may help you look and feel your best during everyday occasions. They're great for touch-ups on the go.

9:2 Capturing the Essence of Everyday Runway Beauty

The key to everyday runway beauty is to feel secure and at ease in your skin. It's about embracing your distinctive traits and enhancing your natural attractiveness with hair and makeup.

How to capture the essence of everyday runway beauty:

1: Flawless Skin: Begin with a flawless foundation. To create a smooth canvas and balance out your skin tone, use a primer, foundation, or BB cream. Choose a natural finish versus one with lots of covering.

2: Fresh and Dewy: Use a moisturizing serum or mist to get a fresh, dewy complexion. For a beautiful glow, emphasize the high features of your face, such as your cheekbones and brow bone.

3: Bold Brows: A runway-inspired beauty look requires well-groomed, defined eyebrows to frame the face. Any bare spots should be filled in with a brow pencil or powder.

4: Statement Eyes: Adopt striking eye makeup. Try experimenting with vivid eyeshadows, graphic eyeliner, or dramatic lashes to give your appearance a dash of runway flair.

5: Natural Lips: Natural lips can soften the impact of strong eyes. For a finish that exudes effortless chic, choose neutral or sheer hues of lipstick or lip gloss.

6: Creative Nails: Nail art is quickly becoming popular. To show your creativity and improve your overall appearance, experiment with different nail patterns, colors, and textures.

7: Hair Accessories: To give your hairdo a dash of runway flair, add hair accessories like hairpins, headbands, or scarves.

8: Experiment with Texture: Try disheveled waves or curls as well as sleek and straight hair textures. Changing the texture of your hair can completely alter how you appear.

9: Combine High and Low Fashion: Mix upscale and budget-friendly clothing. This diverse combination can produce a cutting-edge look without going over budget.

10: Individual Style: Stay true to your taste while getting inspiration from the runways. To fit your preferences and comfort level, modify runway trends.

11: Confidence is key. Self-assurance is the icing on the cake. You'll attract attention wherever you go if you carry your everyday runway beauty appearance with confidence.

12: Keep It Practical: Keep in mind that everyday runway beauty needs to be useful in your day-to-day activities. Pick outfits that go with your daily activities and timetable.

13: Experimenting is fun. Don't be scared to try out different looks and styles. Pushing limits and embracing imagination are key components of runway beauty.

14: Make skincare a priority. To ensure that your skin looks its best, follow a healthy skincare routine. Any runway-inspired look looks best on skin that is clear and vibrant.

15: StayStay Informed: For inspiration, follow fashion publications, blogs, or social media accounts to keep up with the latest in fashion and beauty trends.

To showcase your style and capture the essence of everyday runway beauty, you must embrace your inner fashionista. It's a creative and enjoyable method to experiment with various outfits and find high-fashion inspiration while being genuine with oneself.

CONCLUSION

In "Claudia Schiffer's Beauty Secrets: From the Runway to Everyday Life," we travel on a wonderful trip through the life and wisdom of a world-famous fashion figure. The life of Claudia Schiffer is one of change, passion, and the enduring attraction of beauty that extends beyond the catwalk and melds into regular life.

Claudia's path has been nothing short of incredible, from her early years spent growing up in Rheinberg, Germany, through her quick ascension to supermodel dom and her enduring influence on the fashion industry.Her experience is proof that anyone, anywhere in the world, can achieve beauty. It is not just a trait reserved for the glitzy world of fashion shows and glossy magazines.

The skincare regimens, cosmetic techniques, and haircare rituals that have enabled Claudia to preserve an ageless radiance have all been covered in this book. We've looked into her diet and exercise regimen and learned that true beauty comes from having a healthy body and mind. Claudia has emphasized the value of inner peace and the transformative potential of mindfulness, illuminating the way to both inner and outer brilliance.

We've also learned about Claudia's persistent sense of style, how her taste has changed over the years and the pieces in her wardrobe that help her feel confident every day. Anyone looking to show their individuality via dress can use her classic fashion selections as a guide.

Claudia's knowledge has offered time-saving tips for busy lives in the field of quick beauty repairs and beauty hacks. All those looking to incorporate the essence of runway-inspired beauty into their daily routines now have access to these tips and tactics, which are based on her experience as a supermodel.

As we come to an end, keep in mind that Claudia Schiffer's beauty goes beyond the surface and is a reflection of her distinct attitude, self-assurance, and classic style. Her legacy stands as a beacon of inspiration for anybody wishing to embrace their beauty and lead a confident, graceful life.

Accept the life lessons Claudia learned on the runway, and let her insight inspire you to recognize and appreciate your beauty. As Claudia has demonstrated, beauty is a journey that may be filled with joy, confidence, and a sense of limitless potential.